To Mrs. Perron,

God bless you and
give you peace.

your friend,
Fr. Ulmer Kuhn O.F.M.
May 14, 1974

ÁCOMA

In the first week of September 1540, Captain Hernando de Alvarado entered in his journal: ". . .found a rock with a village on top, the strongest position in all the land, well fortified, the best there is in Christiandom". Sent forward by his commander, Francisco Vasquez de Coronado, the Spanish captain was thus the first white man in recorded history to see strange, beautiful, mysterious Ácoma, the sky city.

The pueblo of Ácoma and the 350-foot precipitous sandstone mesa upon which it rests, has always been one of the most interesting places in New Mexico. From the earliest of exploring travelers until today, this ancient "sky city" has never failed to fascinate visitors. Geographically, it is removed from the mainstream of travel, being situated in the heart of "mesa land". One drives west from Albuquerque for perhaps 46 miles, then turns into the mesa country for 16 more miles. It is not a difficult drive, but it is a time-consuming drive.

The Ácoma of today has changed but little since the visit of Captain Alvarado in 1540.

LITHO BY WALSWORTH PUB. CO., INC., MARCELINE, MO.

H. L. JAMES

ÁCOMA

The People of the White Rock

Introduction by FRANK WATERS

The Rio Grande Press, Inc.

GLORIETA, NEW MEXICO · 87535

A short article on this subject, by author

Frank Waters, using several of the photographs

reproduced in this book, was published in

the July/August 1970 issue of

NEW MEXICO MAGAZINE.

A RIO GRANDE PRESS PICTORIAL SPECIAL

LIBRARY OF CONGRESS CARD CATALOG 72-139224

I.S.B.N. 87380-072-9

First printing 1970

The Rio Grande Press, Inc.

GLORIETA, NEW MEXICO · 87535

Publisher's Preface

For eight years we have worked towards the goal of publishing a new book, and finally, here it is. Lovely as the book is, though, it does poor justice to the reality. All of New Mexico is beautiful, but the land at and around Ácoma is especially beautiful. The windswept miles, the majestic and colorful clouds in an azure sky, the red earth counterpointing the green trees, the incredible formations of the earth and hills, the whole lovely complex is a sight by itself never to be forgotten.

Then one visits, amidst all this soul-stirring scenery, ancient Ácoma. It is to move from the modern world backward to a land that time forgot, perhaps a thousand years or more. There is nothing like it anywhere in America.

The citizens of Ácoma are a handsome people, sturdy, resourceful, independent and proud. Theirs is a marvelous history, alive on all sides with the evidences of antiquity. Their traditions are a living mythology, and still a secret from those who do not belong. Ácoma and its people are something very special to see and visit.

And to respect.

Robert B. McCoy

La Casa Escuela
Glorieta, N. M.
November 1970

Introduction

A jagged old molar sticking up from the toothless plain—this is the great Rock of Acuco, the Peñol of Ácoma, sixty miles west of Albuquerque and fourteen miles south of U. S. 66. And perched on its flat top, 357 feet high, about the height of a 40-story skyscraper, the pueblo colorfully called the "Sky City".

Captain Hernando de Alvarado of Coronado's expedition of 1540, the first European of record to see it, reported that he ". . . found a rock with a village on top, the strongest position ever seen in the world," naming it Acuco. It is generally assumed that Ácoma derives its name from Akome, "people of the white rock" as the people call themselves, although the root Ako has no known etymology.

It was long ago, according to their migration myth, when the people were wandering the earth to find a home. The spirits, the kachinas, told them the place would be called Ako. Masewi and Oyoyewi, the sacred twins, were leading the people. So every so often Masewi would stop and call out: "A-a-a-ko-o-o!" There was no answer, and the people wandered on. One day they stopped in front of a huge white rock. "Aaaakoooo-o-o!" Masewi called out in a loud voice, and the rock echoed it back clear and strong. "This is Ako!" he announced. So the people settled at the foot of the east point of the mesa, still called Ako-hai'titu. Then after a council they moved up on top.

Tradition persists that some of the people first lived on top of Katzimo, the "Enchanted Mesa," another nearby and precipitous

7

butte seventy-three feet higher. When a storm blocked the path to it by a.landslide, they moved to this forbidding cliff-rock with the others.

This Keres pueblo of Ácoma in New Mexico contends with the Hopi pueblo of Oraibi in Arizona for the distinction of being the oldest continuously-occupied settlement in the United States. Oraibi today is virtually an archaeological ruin of falling walls in which live scarcely a dozen families. Ácoma, in contrast, is a well-kept village regarded as home by 2,750 people, half of whom live on the reservation; the second largest tribal group of New Mexico's eighteen Indian pueblos. Throughout its long and tempestuous history it has had the will to live and it still has.

How ancient the pueblo is no one knows. Certainly it long antedates the first settlement of English Pilgrims in 1620 marked by an inconspicuous boulder on the Atlantic shore of Plymouth harbor. Sherds found at Ácoma indicate the site has been occupied for at least a thousand years.

. In prehistoric times the people lived as a self-contained unity on their lofty mesa between the immeasurable expanse of sky and the vast empty plain seamed with low outcrops of rock and long cañadas dark with juniper. So it is easy for us today to speak of the people as a collective unity enduring as an unbroken continuity through the centuries. The old died, the new were born. But the communal pattern remained the same. In little *milpas* below their home rock they cultivated corn, squash, beans and cotton, and raised flocks of turkeys. The crops were dependent upon rain, and during drouths the people suffered. Gradually they ventured six leagues north to a place now called Cubero. It lay in a cañada perhaps a league long and half a league wide, watered by a little stream. Here they could irrigate their crops.

Occasionally enemies came: "Apaches so insolent," reported a later Spanish priest, "that if this pueblo were not by nature defensible, perhaps nothing would now remain of it." The Ácomas then fled to the summit of their mesa, climbing tortuous trails formed by ladders and toe-and-finger holes cut into the rock, and hurling down boulders and rocks upon their pursuers.

On top they were prepared to withstand a long siege. The bare flat sandstone comprised barely seventy acres. It was split in half by a deep, narrow cleft. To the north stood three parallel blocks of communal buildings of two or three stories each, built of stones and adobe. Since there was no soil on the rocky surface, all the earth used to make adobe had to be carried in buffalo-hide bags up from the plain.

The only water on top was preserved in natural cisterns in the bedrock. Fray Francisco Atanasio Dominguez in 1776 described the largest on the south half of the mesa as "a cistern which God made in the rock itself. Its opening must be about forty varas in circumference, and it must be fully as deep. Rain water is caught in it, and when it snows the Indians take care to collect all the snow they can . . . In order that the rain water may be clean when it goes in, they are careful to keep the space around it swept, and there is a guard to prevent pollution. The water collected in this usually half fills it. Because the rock is solid, it has never been known to become fetid, and is always fresh although turbid."

The first change came with the Spaniards. Coronado's discovery expedition of 1540 was followed by the *Entrada* of Espejo and other small parties. Not until 1598 did Juan de Oñate make the first successful effort to colonize the country. His impressive train comprised 400 men and their families, eighty-three baggage carts and 7,000 head of stock. Receiving the obediencias of many pueblos on the Rio Grande, he dispatched Don Juan de Zaldivar with thirty-one men to Ácoma in the "Kingdom of Acus." It was then Ácoma gained the reputation of being the most treacherous and intractable of all pueblos.

On December 1, 1598, Zaldivar reached the great fortress and camped two leagues away. Three days later, with eighteen men, he ascended the rock to get some cornmeal the Indians had promised him. Without warning, the chief Zutucapan and his warriors attacked the Spanish detachment. Zaldivar and twelve of his men were killed, the survivors escaping back to Oñate.

Oñate then dispatched another force of seventy men under Juan de Zaldivar's brother, Vicente, to avenge his brother's death and punish Ácoma. Included in the detachment was the soldier-poet Gaspar Perez de Villagrá.

Their assault of the "Sky City" began on January 22, 1599, and lasted three days. While most of the soldiers engaged the Indians at the ladder trails, Villagrá with twelve men gained the summit of the south section separated from the village area by the deep cleft in the rock. With a celebrated leap, Villagrá cleared the chasm and threw logs across to bridge it. Then he and his companions joined the main force hacking its way into the pueblo.

The Spaniards burned the town, killing more than 600 Ácomas and taking nearly 600 prisoners. Some seventy captured warriors were confined in a kiva. From here they were taken out one by one, murdered, and thrown over the cliff. The remaining 500 captives, most of them women and children, Zaldivar marched to Santo Domingo to stand trail. Here in February Oñate, finding them guilty of killing eleven Spaniards and their two servants, pronounced sentence. All males of more than twenty-five years of age were condemned to have one foot cut off and to give twenty years of personal service to the Spaniards; the males between twelve and twenty-five years, and all females, were doomed to servitude.

This conquest of Ácoma was celebrated by Villagrá's epic poem, *The History of New Mexico,* published in Spain in 1610. Villagrá himself transported sixty or seventy of the young captive girls to the viceroy in Mexico. It is an interesting corollary that his daughter married the grandnephew of Moctezuma, the last Aztec emperor of Mexico, conquered by Cortez; and that Oñate himself married the great-granddaughter of Moctezuma. These two men thus helped to father the nucleus of a new mixed race of Spanish-Indian blood on the American continent, the mestizo.

Oñate's colonization of New Mexico seemed well established under harsh Spanish rule. Every pueblo household was required to pay in tribute one vara (thirty-three inches) of cotton cloth. Indians were flogged for infringement of the laws. People were enslaved to labor for the Crown and the Church, and their native worship was regarded as idolatry.

Ácoma stubbornly survived under this regime. Then in 1629 Fray Juan Ramirez was escorted to the pueblo by the governor of New Mexico, Francisco Manuel Silva Nieto, as its first permanent missionary. Father Ramirez was a stout Franciscan. Envisioning a church on the citadel, he built a trail to the top named after him *El Camino del Padre,* "The Path of the Father." He then directed the building of the so-called Burro Trail which could be used for packing up materials for the erection of the church.

There is some controversy today as to just when the church was built. Consensus is that it was constructed by Father Ramirez between 1629 and 1641. The church was dedicated to the first martyr San Estevan, St. Stephen, the original patron saint of Ácoma. But as his feast day came on December 26, coinciding with Christmas, the celebration was later changed to the feast day of St. Stephen, the King of Hungary, on September 2, the church taking the name of San Estevan Rey.

Construction was extremely difficult. Embracing an area 150 feet long and forty feet wide, the walls were sixty feet high and ten feet thick. The great logs for the roof vigas, forty feet long and fourteen inches square, were cut in the Cebolleta Mountains thirty miles away. Building the adjoining cemetery was another feat. A rock retaining wall forty feet high was constructed on the edge of the mesa, and the 200-foot square was filled with earth, all this material being hauled up from the valley below.

Meanwhile, during its construction, Indian rebellion against the

Spanish crown was being slowly organized by Popé, a medicine-man working from Taos Pueblo. On August 10, 1680, every pueblo rebelled, the Ácomas murdering Fray Luis Maldonado Olasqueain, the current priest. In all, the Indians killed nearly 500 Spaniards, including twenty-one friars at their altars, tore down churches, destroyed government and church records, "vented their fury on the hens, the sheep, the fruit trees of Castile, and even upon the wheat," and washed the heads of all baptized Indians to cleanse them of the Spanish stain. The surviving Spaniards fled back to Mexico.

Again in 1692 a new wave of conquest rolled in with Don Diego de Vargas Zapata y Lujan, Ponce de Leon on its crest. This time De Vargas with much diplomacy promised forgiveness to all pueblos which would submit to Spanish rule. He then marched westward with his small army. In November 1693 he reached a spring, *El Pozo,* from which he could see the Peñol of Ácoma. As he wrote in his journal: "We described the smoke made by those traitors, enemies, treacherous rebels, and apostates of the Zueres (Keres) tribe." Finally, with much persuasion, he induced them to parley. But not until 1699 did Ácoma formally submit to Spanish rule.

The advantages soon became apparent to the Ácomas. The Spaniards were introducing horses, cattle and sheep, fruit trees, new customs, and a new faith. So after nearly two centuries there began that amalgamation of Spanish and Indian cultures which characterizes New Mexico today.

The Ácomas today are almost wholly devout Catholics. Almost every Ácoma bears a Spanish name. But none of them speak Spanish, as do the pueblos along the Rio Grande.

The coming of the "Americans" brought another, shorter period of change. Following General Stephen W. Kearny's bloodless march of conquest from the Missouri to Santa Fe, and the war between Mexico and the United States, all of New Mexico was ceded by Mexico to the United States by the Treaty of Guadalupe Hidalgo in 1848.

Spain in 1551, under King Charles V, had provided land grants to each pueblo with water rights, farming lands and mountains. This law was confirmed by the Royal Council of the Indies on June 4, 1687. Mexico, after winning independence from Spain in 1824, had in turn confirmed the pueblos' titles to their communally-owned land grants. And now, the United States in 1858 was the third nation to confirm the Ácoma title to its land.

Five years later Ácoma sent its governor with those of six other pueblos to visit President Abraham Lincoln in Washington. Settling boundaries to their grants, President Lincoln presented each governor with a silver-headed cane as a token of their right to govern their own affairs. On the cane presented to the governor of Ácoma was engraved:

A. Lincoln,
Prst., U. S. A.,
Ácoma
1863

This cane was passed to each succeeding governor when he was elected in January, constituting his badge of office. Governor Sam Victorino today still carries the cane to all official functions.

Frank Waters

Taos, N. M.
November 1970

(Mr. Frank Waters is one of New Mexico's most distinguished literary figures, and is the author of numerous books about the Southwest. Probably the best known of his books is The Man Who Killed the Deer.)

To
ROSE ANN

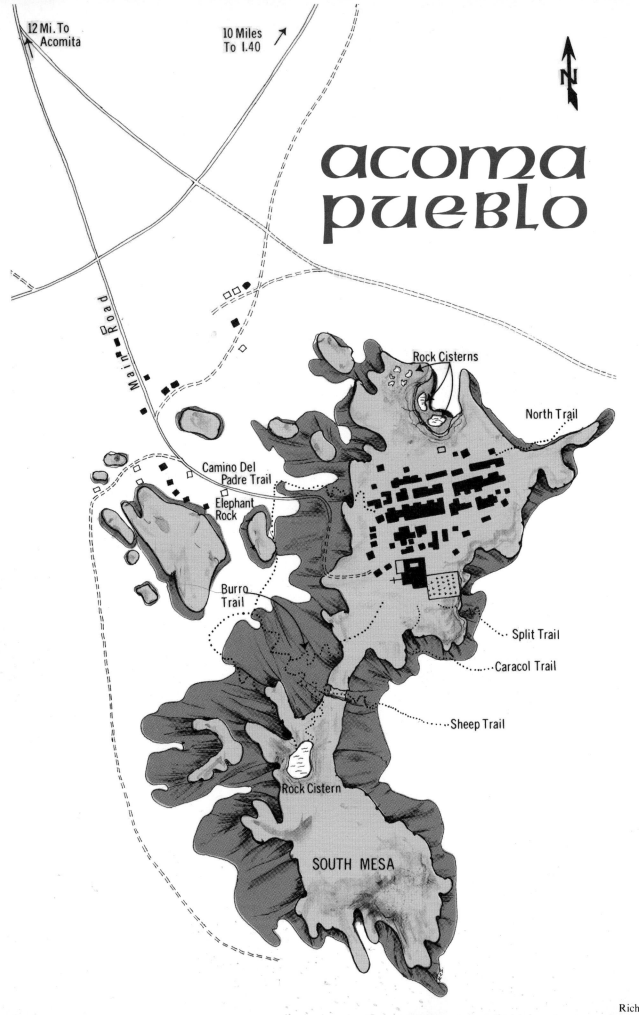

12 Mi. To Acomita

10 Miles To I.40

acoma pueblo

N

Main Road

Rock Cisterns

North Trail

Camino Del Padre Trail

Elephant Rock

Burro Trail

Split Trail

Caracol Trail

Sheep Trail

Rock Cistern

SOUTH MESA

Richard Sandoval

CONTENTS

THE PLACE   16

THE PEOPLE   56

THEIR WAY OF LIFE   64

KATZIMO   82

THE PLACE • •

There is one Ácoma. It is a class by itself. The peer of it is not in the world. I might call it the Queres Gibraltar; but Gibraltar is a pregnable place beside it. It is the Quebec of the Southwest; but Quebec could be stormed in the time an army climbed Ácoma unopposed. If as a defensible town there be no standard whereby to measure it, comparison is still more hopeless when we attack its impregnable beauty and picturesqueness. It is the Garden of the Gods multiplied by ten, and with ten equal but other wonders thrown in; plus a human interest, an archaeological value, an atmosphere of romance and mystery. It is the labyrinth of wonders of which no person alive knows all, and of which not six white men have even an adequate conception, though hundreds have seen it in part. The longest visit never wears out its glamour: one feels as in a strange, sweet, unearthly dream, whose very rocks are genii, and whose people swart conjurors. It is the spendthrift of beauty.

Lummis
Land of Poco Tiempo
P. 57

". . . found a rock with a village
on top, the strongest position that
ever was seen in the world, which
was called A′cuco in their language

Alvarado
Acoma, the Sky City
Sedgwick
P. 60

. . . It is one of the strongest places
we have seen, because the city is on
a very high rock with a rough ascent,
so that we repented háving gone up
to the place.

Alvarado, quoted in
A'coma, the Sky City
Sedgwick
P. 59

The village was very strong, because it was up on a rock out of reach, having steep sides in every direction, and so high that it was a very good musket that could throw a ball as high. There was only one entrance by a stairway built by hand, which began at the top of a slope which is around the foot of the rock. There was a broad stairway for about 200 steps, then a stretch of about 100 narrower steps, and at the top they had to go up about three times as high as a man by means of holes in the rock, in which they put the points of their feet, holding on at the same time with their hands. There was a wall of large and small stones at the top, which they could roll down without showing themselves, so that no army could possibly be strong enough to capture the village.

Casteñada, 1540
The Coronado Expedition
George Parker Winship
P. 215

No storm-tossed mariner ever viewed a friendly port with more delight than did the savage Ácomans behold our troops. No sooner had they sighted us than they raised a howl of delight, so loud, so fierce, so terrible, that it seemed as if hell had turned loose all its demons.

Marching thus in orderly fashion we reached the powerful fortress. It seemed impregnable, consisting of two lofty rocks, over three hundred paces apart, rising from the plain to an imposing height. These two cliffs were joined by a ridge of jagged rocks. A narrow pathway connected the two, broken in several places by deep crevasses. We had never before seen such a stupendous mass of malformed rock, rising from the air and towering upward almost into the skies, it seemed.

From this lofty haven Zutacapán watched our men as they filed past, counting each one. Seeing us so few in numbers, he danced with glee and with a well-satisfied smile on his face spoke thus to his men: "They are here. What fool-hardiness! These are simpletons indeed to have walked into such danger with a mere handful of men".

Gicombo answered him: "They may be fools, but I say the world has never before seen a like number of such fools. See them; they come in such small numbers, but they appear determined. Notice how they are looking us over. There is some great mystery here".

Then Zutancalpo spoke: "We will well know that these strangers have come from far and distant lands. Who knows the distance they have traveled, and the dangers and conflicts they have met? Yet they come before us so few in numbers. Undoubtedly they have many times before this given proof of their strength and valor".

Zutacapán interrupted him, saying that he needed no assistance. He asked only to be permitted to begin the attack and reap for himself the good fortune which had come to him. He called to his men. They leaped forward like so many unleashed greyhounds. Some were clad in many-colored blankets; other were dressed in skins and wore masks. Among the warriors were many maidens of surpassing beauty, stark naked. Secure in their eyrie castle they taunted the Spaniards, exhibiting their naked bodies with neither modesty nor shame. Many of the savages were also naked. They painted their bodies with daubs and stripes of black, red, and white. What a terrible sight they were! A regular troop of imps from hell. They also taunted the Spaniards as they leaped from cliff to cliff, their shaggy

hair hanging in mats and dragging the long tails and horns
of their costumes.

Villagra
History of New Mexico
P. 221-222

At early daybreak, Father Fray Alonso (Martinez) celebrated Holy Mass. It was the feast of his saint's day. All the soldiers devoutly received communion. After the Mass the father spoke to them as follows: "Knights of Christ, strong in battle, defenders of the Holy Faith, it is needless for me to recommend the safety of our Holy cause to your brave arms, for, as noble sons of the Holy Church you have always served her well. I do beseech you, however, through Christ our Savior, to restrain your bloody arms as much as you can, lest needless blood may flow. The true valor of Catholic arms is to conquer without death or bloodshed. Go in Christ's name, In his Holy name I bless you one and all."

We then made our way to the first rock and scaled its walls. When we arrived at the summit, we were surprised to note the pueblo was to all appearances deserted and abandoned. Such was the eagerness of our men that, without awaiting orders, some of them bridged the first span which broke the pathway and thirteen of our men rushed across.

The thirteen had hardly crossed when Gicombo and his men were attacking them with spirit. Like a wounded whale which, dragging the sharp harpoon in its side, lashes the sea from side to side with its enormous tail, spouting water high into the air, and then leaps almost out of the water, causing the sea to boil and rage in a thousand whirlpools, so did Gicombo struggle. They were almost upon our men, so they immediately fired the powerful arquebuses, killing a great number of the Indians. But this did not stop them, and our men, having no time to reload, drew their swords and opposed them hand to hand.

We on the opposite side of the crevasse could not assist our comrades, for in their haste to proceed they had pulled up again the beam to carry it with them and use it at other places. The Spaniards met the foe with gallant efforts, causing terrible havoc among them with their sharp blades: Here a skull was opened wide, here a throat was cut from ear to ear, here an arm, here a leg dismembered. Foremost among them were the two brothers Cristóbal and Francisco Sánchez, Captain Quesada, Juan Piñero, Francisco Vázquez, Manuel Francisco, Cordero, Juan Rodriguez, Pedraza, and others. Like the fingers of the hand, although they are unequal in strength and size, still when they are clinched and grasp an object they are all united and equal, so these comrades all united in one mighty effort against the many savages who opposed them. Blood flowed like water; their swords dripped gore from the very hilts.

Carrasco, Isasti, Casas, and Montesinos proved their worth in this encounter. They fought together, and many were the luckless savages who fell beneath the blow of their gallant swords.

At this point Zutancalpo and Buzcoico came to reinforce the savages with a great number of men. The Spaniards retreated to a natural cave, where, entrenched against the savages, they held them at bay, safe from their arrows and the many missiles which rained upon them. They easily held them at a distance with their arquebuses.

The sergeant cried out for someone to bring another log to bridge the span. Thinking he was talking to me, I stepped back nine paces, running toward the edge of the chasm, and like Circio, with a terrible leap left the edge. The sergeant had sought to stop me, but missed his hold. Had he not, that day would most certainly have been my last upon this earth. My depression lent me wings, and I landed safely on the other side, where I frantically seized the beam and bridged the crevasse. The trumpeter blew a blast and our soldiers dashed across. When our comrades heard this and saw us coming, they emerged from their trench like the dead on judgment day when they shall come forth from their sepulchers to answer Gabriel's final call.

Seeing that defeat had changed to victory, our men now attacked with vigor . . .

For three days the battle raged. The Spaniards neither ate nor drank nor slept during all this time. The houses were almost all ablaze or burned to the ground. Dense columns of smoke poured forth from the windows as from the mouth of a volcano. The unhappy savages, seeing that all was lost, threw themselves in numbers into the raging flames. Some leaped to their death from the top of the Rock; others turned their arms upon one another, father slew son, and son slew father.

When Gicombo and Bempol saw that all was lost, they determined to die together. Some of their comrades sought to dissuade them, urging them to surrender to the Castilians. To these Gicombo answered:

"Unworthy A'comans, what has come to pass that you offer such unworthy advice? What is left for you once these Castilians are victorious and have you in their power? We have reached the final point where, without liberty, it is better that we were dead. Could we endure life under such conditions? O, A'coma, once you were great and mighty. Those very gods who lifted you to this high glory have now deserted you, and see to what ignoble depths you have fallen! Remember your oath, A'comans! Did you not solemnly promise that if victory were denied us, you would all sooner perish than surrender your honor? Death is a thousand times more welcome than a life of infamy and disgrace."

Neither Maximinus, Macrinus, Maxentius, Procrustes, Diocletian, Tiberius nor Nero ever showed such cruelty as did these savages as they began to turn their arms upon one another. Not only the men, but the women, followed his advice. Some, like the abandoned Dido, hurled themselves to their destruction; others died by fire like Portia; others turned sharp daggers to their breasts like a Lucretia.

Villagrá
History of New Mexico
P. 242, 243, 244, 249, 250

If there is any sight in the world which will cling to one, undimmed by later impressions, it is the first view of Ácoma from the mesa as one comes in from the west. After the long, slow slope among the sprawling cedars, one stands suddenly upon a smooth divide; looking out upon such a scene as is nowhere else. A few rods ahead, the mesa breaks down in a swift cliff of six hundred feet to a valley that seems surely enchanted. A grassy trough, five miles wide and ten in visible length, smooth with that ineffable hazy smoothness which is only of the Southwest, crowded upon by noble precipices, patched with exquisite hues of rocks and clays and growing crops - it is such a vista as would be impossible outside the arid lands. And in its midst lies a shadowy world of crags so unearthly beautiful, so weird, so unique, that it is hard for the onlooker to believe himself in America, or upon this dull planet at all. As the evening shadows play hide-and seek among those towering sandstones it is as if an army of Titan marched across the enchanted plain.

To the left beetles the vast cliff of Kat-zi-mo, or the Mesa Encantada, the noblest single rock in America; to the right, the tall portals of two fine cañons, themselves treasure-houses of wonders; between, the chaos of the buttes that flank the superb mesa of Ácoma. That is one rock - a dizzy air-island above the plain - three hundred and fifty-seven feet high, seventy acres in area upon its irregular but practically level top - a stone table upheld by ineffable precipices which are not merely perpendicular but in great part actually overhanging.

Lummis
Land of Poco Tiempo
P. 58

Upon the bare-table top of
this strange stone island of
the desert, seven thousand
feet above the level of the
sea, stands a town of
matchless interest - the
home of half a thousand
quaint lives, and of half a
thousand years' romance.

Lummis
Land of Poco Tiempo
P. 61

The contour of those cliffs is an endless enchantment. They are broken by scores of marvelous bays, scores of terrific columns and pinnacles, crags, and towers. There are dozens of "natural bridges", from one of a fathom's span to one so sublime, so crushing in its savage and enormous grandeur, that the heart fairly stops beating at first sight of it. There are strange standing rocks, vast potreros and fairy minarets, wonderlands of recesses, and

mysterious caves. It is the noblest specimen of fantastic erosion on the continent. Everywhere there is insistent suggestion of Assyrian sculpture in its rocks. One might fancy it a giant Babylon, water-worn to dimness. The peculiar cleavage of its beautiful sandstone has hemmed it with strange top-heavy statues that guard grim chasms.

Lummis
Land of Poco Tiempo
P. 58-61

When seen from below, the outer walls of the dwellings seem to be part of the mesa itself, merely hewn from the solid rock. Closely approached, they are found to be as much fortress as house. Three parallel lines of stone and adobe, a thousand feet long and forty feet high, running east and west, are separated from one another by calles or streets of moderate width - the calle between the middle row and the south row being left wider than the others, to provide a plaza for open-air ceremonials.

Each of these structures consists of three storeys built in terraces, after a fashion common enough in the pueblo country. The lowest storey is between twelve and fifteen feet high, and had originally no openings save trap doors on the top. It was used exclusively for the storage of supplies, enough of which could be kept there to withstand a long siege. The Ácomas therefore enter their houses by ladders from the ground to the second storey, but the third storey and the roofs are reached by steep and narrow steps on the division walls. In all terraced pueblos, economy of construction was one feature of this type of house. A far more important consideration was necessity for mutual defense, felt by every small community exposed to raids. No one could forsee when would appear a roving band of hostile Navajos, Apaches or Comanches, but their forced tribute upon the crops at some time was as certain as the dawning of the day.

Though in appearance these long blocks of apartments are community houses, they are in no sense communal if that term be used to define a socialistic form of life. Each family or clan is a unit completely separated from every other by very solid division walls. Independence of all but the immediate family or clan can hardly be carried to a greater extreme than with the Indian. Injury or insult, even if sometimes imaginary, may provoke tragic results; silent and wary by nature, and made suspicious by experience, the Indian is indifferent to the well-being of his neighbor across streets as narrow as those that separate the house-blocks of Ácoma, and he asks an equal privacy for himself.

Sedgwick
Ácoma, The Sky City
P. 19-20

Here and there, in hidden corners, are bee-hive-like ovens, by the side of which are great piles of cedar wood, and interesting it is to see the busy housewifes at their cooking and baking. The fire is made in the oven and allowed to burn down to the hottest kind of coals. These are then scraped out, the oven floor hastily swept or mopped out, and the bread or meat to be baked thrust inside. Then a slab or rock is placed as a door and its edges plastered with mud so that no heat or vapours can escape. When the food is taken out no chef in the well-equipped kitchen of a modern hotel can find fault with the way the oven has performed its function.

George Wharton James
The Land of The Delight Makers
P. 130-131

We traveled through a level valley, in which we saw many flocks of sheep grazing, attended by Indian pastores and their ever-watchful dogs. I tried to purchase some sheep from the people, who were guarding them, but I could not induce them to make any bargin until a chief, attended by some eight or ten Indians, rode up. He appeared to be a wealthy man, and we soon agreed about the purchase.

After a journey of fifteen miles we arrived at Ácoma. On the northern side of the rock, the rude boreal blasts have heaped up the sand, so as to form a practical ascent for some distance; the rest of the way is through solid rock. At one place a singular opening, or narrow way, is formed between a huge square tower of rock and the perpendicular face of the cliff. At one place just after passing the narrow defile, near the tower rock, a wall has been raised by the Indians to prevent accidents - from persons falling over the precipice . . .

J. W. Abert
New Mexico Report 1846-47
P. 82-88

Doubtless no other town in the world to-day is still reached by such dizzy trails as Ácoma...

The Camino del Padre is by far the most frequently used. Big flat stones have been lodged so as to afford rude steps in the lower gulch; and at one point one must climb fly-like up one cliff-side by toe-holds, and directly pass under a huge fallen boulder from above, caught in the jaws of the cliff; and, climbing up a big notched log, crawl through a narrow opening at the other side of this opening.

Lummis
Mesa, Canon, And Pueblo
P. 197-198

Then there is the "Burro Trail", which we concluded is the one built under the inspiration of Father Ramirez, so that a comfortable pathway from the plain might be possible for man and beast. At its head is a good-sized wooden cross which still on Cross Day, in May, is decorated with flowers and before which the people used to kneel to receive a blessing from the bishop during his annual visit.

Sedgwick
A'coma, The Sky City
P. 29

But the gem of all the ancient adits to Ácoma is the wild "North Trail." Thi[s]
attacks the highest part of the cliff behind the back walls of the northern row [o]
houses. Starting at the foot with a notched log, winding around a dome of san[d]
stone by single footholds barely wide enough to receive a foot, and with no alte[r]
native if you put the wrong foot forward, it clambers past a natural bridge an[d]
into a tremendous rocky amphitheater of overpowering majesty, in which si[t]
enthroned a colossal, awesome figure like a buddha. It is all very well until with[
in the last hundred feet of the top; there the trail peters out into a narrow shel[f]
sloping outward, where you must cling to the finger-holds in the cliff as you edg[e]
along sideways and can look down over your shoulder hundreds of feet. And th[e]
last forty feet are straight up, with toe-holds on either side of a narrow clef[t]

The Indians have not used this trail for a century, not merely because it is difficult and dangerous, but because it is "haunted". Long ago, on one feast day, there was a race to climb this trail - a man carrying a sheep on his shoulders, and a woman a tinaja of water on her head. The sheep kicked just as the young brave came midway of the last ladder rock and threw its bearer down backwards; he fell upon the woman, and all rolled down the cliff to mutilation.

Lummis
Mesa, Cañon, and Pueblo
P. 198-199

There are no dwellings on the southern mesa; but thither leads—down the side of the crag- hyphen and up again — a trail, deep worn in the rock, to the great reservoir, chief of the many hollows which serve Ácoma for water-works. This reservoir - a picturesquely beautiful cavity in the solid rock - should be seen at sunrise, when the strange lights and shadows, the clear image of its bluff walls in the mirror of a lake- let make it a vision never to be forgotten.

Lummis
Land of Poco Tiempo
P. 72

Every drop of water used in the houses is brought by the women in three to five gallon tinajas upon their heads - an exercise which may be largely responsible for the superb necks and chests and the confident poise of head notable among all Pueblo women. There is no more picturesque sight than the long file of these comely maids and matrons marching homeward in the sunset glow with their careless head-burdens.

Lummis
Land of Poco Tiempo
P. 72

Thirty years later there was another capture of A'-coma, as remarkable and as heroic as Zaldivar's marvelous assault, but with other weapons. In that year of 1629 came the apostle of the A'comas, brave, gentle Fray Juan Ramirez, walking his perilous way alone from distant Santa Fé. His new parishioners received him with a storm of arrows. There is a current legend that they threw him off the cliff, and that his priestly robes upheld him miraculously and saved his life; but this is a myth without foundation of fact. It probably sprang, partly, from confusion with the marvelous and real escape of Onate's four men who leaped over the cliff and lived, and partly from a misunderstanding of the Indian folk-lore. The undaunted Franciscan faced the wrath of the savages, and finally won their hearts. For a score of years he lived alone among them, taught them to read and write, and led them to Christianity. The first church in A'coma, built two centuries and a half ago, was one of the monuments of this as noble and successful missionary as ever lived.

Lummis
Land of Poco Tiempo
P. 66-67

An impression prevails that the present edifice is not in any part the original one of Ramirez, but one built after the reconquest in 1699 or 1700. . .

. . .but in substance we can visit to-day the basilica of Ramirez.

Sedgwick
A'coma, The Sky City
P. 34-35

The church walls are sixty feet high and ten feet through; and the building covers more ground than any modern cathedral in the United States. The graveyard in front, nearly two hundred feet square, took forty years in the building; for first the gentle toilers had to frame a giant box with stone walls, a box forty feet deep at the outer edges, and then to fill it backful by backful with earth from the far plain.

Lummis
Land of Poco Tiempo
P. 62

There are of course no seats, and the only decoration of the nave is a crude red dado of paint reaching perhaps three feet from the floor. This and the bare white wall above are freshly done each year before the great fiesta of St. Stephen on September second. At the western end the chancel is raised by three shallow steps. Behind the altar is a gaudily painted Mexican scene done in 1802. To the left hangs the miracle-working painting of San José sent to the Mission by Charles II of Spain, it is said.

Sedgwick
A'coma, The Sky City
P. 36

Above the cloister and built upon its corner, there is a charming loggia with a hand-carved wooden railing of simple but attractive design. Here again the view is inspiring, and one likes to fancy those self-sacrificing priests refreshing themselves at the quiet end of day by resting there and taking into their wearied spirits the peace of so healing an aspect of nature.

Sedgwick
A'coma, The Sky City
P. 38

It remains to speak of the great graveyard directly in front of the church,
"where the dead of centuries sleep un-
mindful". It is an enclosure nearly two
hundred feet square, surrounded by a
stone wall plastered with adobe. This
has recently been disfigured by ill-
moulded knob-like heads perhaps a foot

high that stand at regular intervals on its
top. We were told that they were done
during the Great War, and are called
the "soldier guard".

Sedgwick
A'coma, The Sky City
P. 39

Directly in front of us rose two colossal pillars of eroded rock forming a portal through which our eyes were led across the plain to where, over the riven mountain walls, sunlight and an indescribable depth of purple shadow were blending into amethystine haze as the Sun God sank to his rest, just as one has seen it over a boundless ocean. Who can do less at such a moment than join in reverent worship of the Sun?

Sedgwick
A'coma, The Sky City
P. 30

THE PEOPLE

The peole of Ácoma are quaint as their remarkable city. In their very simplicity breathes an atmosphere of the mysterious.

Lummis
Land of Poco Tiempo
P. 69

The costumes of the people are strikingly picturesque, and even handsome. That of the women in particular is Oriental, characteristic, and modest.

Lummis
Land of Poco Tiempo
P. 70

Tangibly they are plain, industrious farmers, strongly
Egyptian in their methods. . .

Lummis
Land of Poco Tiempo
P. 69

THEIR WAY OF LIFE

If we must feel that the Southwest learned from Mexico ". . . how to grow and weave cotton, to irrigate, to build in stone, to obey priests, . . ." we are at the same time impressed by an intrinsic difference in its development and practice from that of Mexico, as we see it in the Pueblo civilization.

Sedgwick
A'coma, The Sky City
P. 176

Although it is possible to regard the current beliefs of the Indian concerning his origin, his migration, and his religion, as largely mythical, all such events are of a grandiose and serious character.

Sedgwick
A'coma, The Sky City
P. 209

The Keres to which the Acomas belong regard Sky Father - synonymous with Sun Father - and Earth Mother as the great deities.

Sedgwick
A'coma, The Sky City
P. 234

From the plumed serpent to the adoration of the bird is an easy transition for the Indian mind. Do we not read in the wisdom of Solomon: "There be three things which are too wonderful for me; and the chief of these were the way of an eagle in the air . . ." And in truth what is more enviable than a bird, that, spurning the earth, may overtop the clouds, pouring out his melody as he soars; or, like the eagle, proud, swift, and sudden, may swoop to clutch his prey and be aloft again in the flash of a moment.

Sedgwick
A'coma, The Sky City
P. 233-234

We know of three important ritual celebrations at Ácoma: namely, the Fiesta of San Estevan, patron saint of the mission and now of the pueblo, on September 2; that of All Souls Day; and the winter solstice rites, commingled with Christmas. A fourth that occurs at the time of the summer solstice, on San Juan's Day, June 24, is in most pueblos an occasion of serious and elaborate ritual...

Sedgwick
Ácoma, The Sky City
P. 253

A'coma's great spectacular game is the gallo race on San Juan's Day, June 24. Some form of this game is found everywhere in New Mexico, among the people of Spanish descent, as well as among the Indians, but the two races play it with difference. At A'coma, the starting point is at the foot of the great mesa. Two old men go out to a level spot at the foot of one of the buttes and plants a cock in the sand so that only his head and perhaps two inches of neck can be seen. I was told that an unusual number of entries were made, and that the men started at the top of the Rock in a foot-race and mounted the horses at the bottom, while running full speed, to catch the fowl and carry it off - "a great race . . .". The victor is pursued by all the others, who tear off bits of feathers and claws or whatever they can secure. The struggle often lasts as much as four hours, the tireless horses and riders, of surpassing agility and endurance, tearing over the broad plain, hither and yon through rock-walled passes, up and over steep ridges of knee-deep sand, rider and horse alike unrecognizable for foam and dust in their wild career.

Sedgwick
A'coma, The Sky City
P. 268-269

And last of all comes the picturesque Tse-ai-tee-ah, the bread-giving. The gallo racers from the plain ride up to the first house in town calling for their reward; then come the maids and matrons from within the second story forth upon the platform-roof of the lower rooms, with flaring great baskets heaped high with gifts of their nutritious bread baked in special ceremonial shapes. And legs of mutton, and tortillas (unleavened pancakes), and pieces of bright calico, and little clingstone peaches, and other articles come hailing down upon the huddled cavalry.

And so from house to every house in the pueblo the cavalcade makes its noisy stages, and at each is received with generous largess.

Lummis
Mesa, Canon, and Pueblo
P. 211

Since the Acoma potters are justly famous, a brief discussion of the ceramic art as practised by the Pueblo peoples is here introduced.

Sedgwick
A'coma, The Sky City
P. 272

The Pueblo people have always dwelt in a land of canyons and high plateaus, rising from great stretches of sand that touch at last the far blue horizon. Here they were provided by nature with an inexhaustible supply of material suitable for pottery. Clay of a consistency perfectly adapted for this purpose is left by the sudden storms that wash through the deep arroyos and deposit therein a valuable sediment. The self-taught potters were not long in learning through experience just what admixture of sand would make this clay malleable and more durable.

Sedgwick
A'coma, The Sky City
P. 275

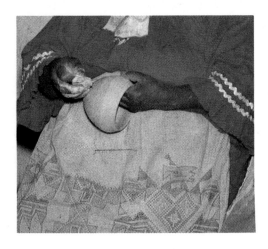

At first, all vessels were probably moulded by the fingers of the potter from a lump of material; then, copying the wicker coils of the basket-maker, the potter rolled in the hands long ropes of clay, mobile and easy to build up spirally into any desired form. Nothing resembling a potter's wheel has ever been employed in the pueblos, but a shallow foot of wicker, or a piece of a gourd often serves as a temporary support in order that the jar may be revolved by a touch of the artist's fingers without injury to the clay coil.

Sedgwick
A'coma, The Sky City
P. 276

After the modelling would come the question whether the irregularities of surface were to be left ribbed or made smooth by scraping with the sharp edge of a bit of gourd, or of a broken shard, or fragment of obsidian.

Sedgwick
A'coma, The Sky City
P. 277

Black appears to have been the first pigment discovered, and the black-and-white pottery is considered the oldest; but it could not be long before an artist living in a land of color would wish to use color on the light surface of the jars, and would begin to reproduce designs familiar in natural objects. Meander patterns and geometric adaptations of rectillinear outlines were employed in an infinite variety of designs. Colors were always used symbolically as well as decoratively on every kind of vessel, whatever its material. Though the work of all pueblo potters is free-hand, it is never haphazard.

Sedgwick
A'coma, The Sky City
P. 277, 278, 280

After the decoration is completed there is the process of firing. The chalk-white clay acquires a mellow tint, varied according to the fuel used. Age, and especially daily use over the fire, deepen and beautify this surface tone so that the older the jar, the more delightful is it to possess.

The better and more usual practice is to dig a little kiln in the ground, or, as is perforce the only way at A'coma, to hollow out a space in the rock. This is lined with dried cakes of sheep dung - now the universal and almost exclusive fuel in all pueblos. The jars are fitted into this shallow kiln and a dome-like structure of dung is built above, after which the whole is slowly fired.

Sedgwick
A'coma, The Sky City
P. 280-281

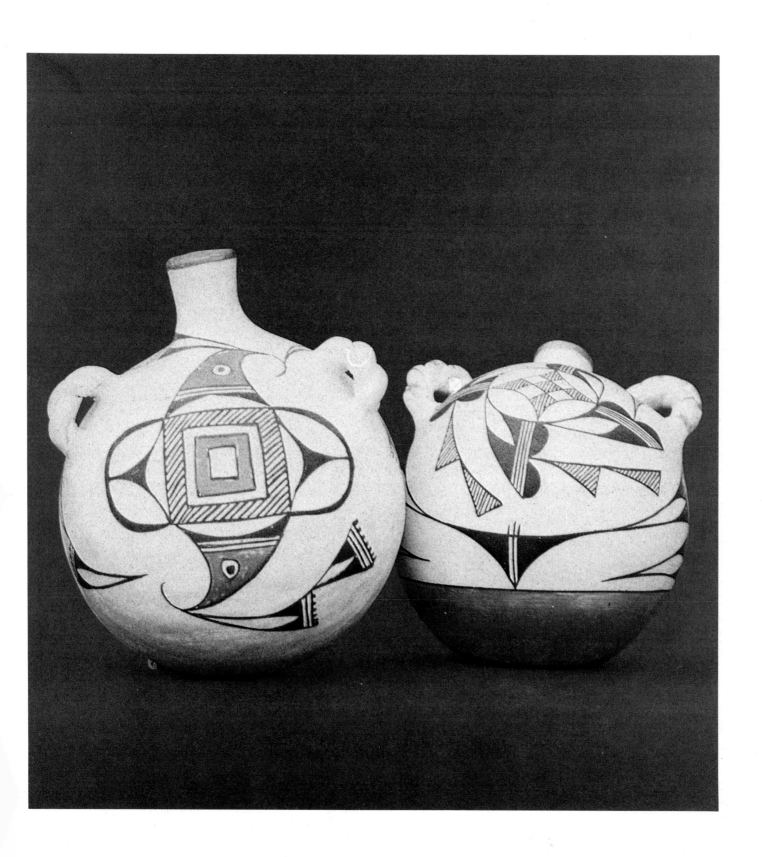

KATZIMO

"Katzimo" - a towering isolated mesa with vertical sides several hundred feet in height and utterly inaccessible. It is one of the most imposing cliffs in that portion of the Southwest and it is claimed by the A'coma Indians that while the top of the mesa is today utterly beyond reach, it was accessible many centuries ago by an easy trail, and that their forefathers had built a pueblo on it after the manner of their present village.

Bandelier, A.A.
Quoted in
A'coma, The Sky City
Sedgwick
P. 166

THE LEGEND OF KATZIMO

BY

H. L. JAMES

No lover of the great Southwest ever doubts an Indian legend. They are always true, though sometimes special meanings are needed in their actual interpretations. One of the most romantic of all the legends is that of Katzimo - the Enchanted Mesa.

The Ácoma Indians relate that many centuries ago their ancestral pueblo lay atop the mesa. The legend states: One day, when all the people were gathering crops in the valley below, there came a great storm that lasted for many days. The force of the water soon undermined the natural rock ladder, the only means of access to the top, causing it to break and come crashing down stranding two old women and a male caretaker named A'-chi-to. When the flood subsided the Ácomas returned from the neighboring highlands and circled the great rock for days, listening to the wails of the despairing on the summit. Councils were held but no way was found to reach the top. The towering walls were inaccessible. Finally it was decided to build a new Ácoma, three miles to the west, on a similar mesa some 100 feet lower in elevation. Here in 1540 Coronado's vanguard found the present site, much as we see it today.

In 1885, New Mexico's famous chronicler, Charles F. Lummis, published the legend and almost at once a bitter controversy broke out. Reading the story, Professor William Libbey of Princeton University set out to discredit the legend as a mere fairy-tale believed only by the foolish and sentimental. It was not until 12 years later, however, that Libbey was able to make a personal examination of the rock. Arriving in the Territory in July, 1897, he procured a small cannon from which he fired a rope over the narrow south end of the mesa. After securing an additional line a block and pulley was instituted, and the professor was hauled to the top in a horsedrawn boatswain's chair. His investigation, although claimed hasty by Lummis, only substantiated his original beliefs that there existed no ruins on Katzimo. On August 28th Professor Libbey released through Harper's weekly an article entitled "A Disenchanted Mesa". The war was on. Lummis, apparently feeling a personal attack on his character as the undisputed authority on the Southwest, countered with a series of articles published in his California-based magazine, *The Land of Sunshine*. No doubt Lummis' feelings were hurt more than anything else by the fact that Libbey had succeeded in being the first white man to conqueror Katzimo, not to mention the unorthodox and ingenious manner in which it was done.

Two weeks later, on September 3, 1897, Frederick Webb Hodge of the Bureau of American Ethnology, took time out from an expedition in Arizona to try and settle the controversy. With the aid of rawhide-tied extension ladders his party ascended through the narrow cleft near the southwest corner of the mesa where legend states the rock stairway once stood. Within a few minutes into the climb Hodge began to pick up a definite trail of continuous hand and toe holds chiseled out along the sandstone ledges. About half way up he encountered a large vertical crack in which was inserted a series of log rungs that fashioned into a crude ladder. On the summit Hodge and his trained assistants found evidence of human occupation in the form of arrow points, pottery flakes, and bead remnants. The subsequent filing of Hodge's report scientifically proved that Katzimo was once inhabited, and that in vindicating the legend, the romance of the Enchanted Mesa still lived.

On June 22, 1898, Charles Lummis wrote: " . . . my own turn came at last. With Hodge's ladder, I took up to the summit, in two hours and ten minutes from the plain. The cruel war is over. Hail Katzimo, the noblest single rock in America".

The following year another writer appeared on the scene and re-opened the verbal battle. George Wharton James wrote in the *Scientific American Supplement* on April 22, 1899, a series of questions which he felt were unanswered on the Ácoma legend. His conclusions were that Katzimo was undoubtedly the scene many times of human presence. The well-worn rock stair steps and other evidences clearly demonstrate that the Indians often visited the summit. However, these signs far misinterpret conclusive evidence that an ancient city of a thousand or two inhabitants dwelt there. In later writings in 1920, James states in his book, *The Land of The Delight Makers,* that actual conversations with Ácoma headsmen revealed that the Enchanted Mesa was not their ancestral home, and that some day he would be escorted to the real, genuine, sole, and only Katzimo, where many ruins are to be found.

Of more recent opinion, the noted archaeologist, Dr. J.W. Fewkes wrote: "I have come to the conclusion that those who hold that the Pueblo once existed on its top have not made their point, archaeologically speaking. That they (Indians) visited the top goes without saying, but to my mind the evidence is more mythical than scientific that any considerable number lived on Katzimo in prehistoric times. The same story is also told by the Navajo of the settlement upon the top of Shiprock. I believe this is one of those legends which are not based wholly upon facts, or at any rate cannot be proven".

ASCENT of the ENCHANTED MESA
(La Mesa Encantada)
BY
·F·W·HODGE·

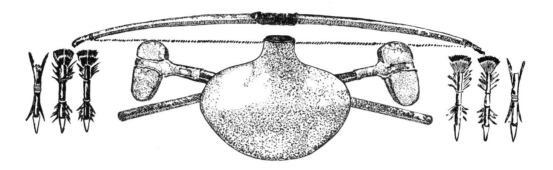

On a rugged rock-table rising from a beautiful level valley in western central New Mexico, the Ácoma Indians have had their home since Francisco Vazquez de Coronado, the commander of the most pretentious army of explorers that ever trod our domain, wended his tedious way in 1540 from Mexico to the bison plains of eastern Kansas.

For how long before the middle of the sixteenth century the natives climbed the dizzy trails that still lead to their eyrie citadel cannot be said; but the Ácomas have an unwritten book of Genesis, which recounts their origin in the mystic under-world of Shipapu, their emergence into this world of light, their migration from the far North, and their fitful settlements for indefinite periods, in similarly indefinite localities, each probably in the hope that the stable middle of this flat, boundless world had at last been found.

We learn this from Ácoma lips; for, like other peoples of prescriptorial culture, these pueblo-dwellers retain mental records of past achievements which are handed down through the ages from father to son, and from shaman to novitiate, even archaic terms and expressions being preserved as they were uttered by the ancients.

The first stopping-place of which the Ácomas have an oral record was Kashkachuti, somewhere in the indefinite North; the next was Washpashuka, southward of the latter, they say; and, traveling still to the southward, as if to seek a more genial clime, they reached a place where the village of Kuchtya was built. The next halt is more definitely located—the Canada de Cruz, at the gateway of which the walls of Tsiama were reared. But the "middle" was not here, it seems; so southward again they journeyed to the beautiful vale of Ácoma, where the pueblo of Tapitsiama was established on a mesa overlooking the valley from the northeast.

Indians do everything with a definite purpose; if they erect a village on a defensive site, it means that they have enemies whose attacks they can thus the better repel. Such a site was Tapitsiama; but it was not impregnable.

A predatory horde may have succeeded in driving out its inhabitants, or it may have been abandoned for other causes. At any rate, the village was deserted, and its Ácoma occupants made another move in their great life-game, this time to the summit of the mighty rock of Katzimo.

Among the peculiarly distinctive natural features that mark New Mexico and Arizona, none is so prominent as the great, flat-topped, steep-sided mesas, or rock-tables, that everywhere rise from the sandy plains throughout the length and breadth of these Territories.

And in this land of mesas, none are more beautiful or more typical than those that hold command over the valley of Ácoma. Their sides are pink and cream, while now and then a splendid dash of purple or crimson suggests the magic stroke of some titanic painter. But the loftiest, most beautiful, most majestic of all is the great isolated table of Katzimo, "la Mesa Encantada" (the Enchanted Mesa), which rises more than four hundred feet from the center of the valley, like an isle of rock from a sea of sand. Its massive walls are adorned with pinnacles and minarets and towering spires, carved by the elements from solid rock, and frescoed in many tints by the same great artists, while on its crest appears a crown of evergreen. The northern and western faces of the escarpment are each relieved by a great cove or amphitheater; but elsewhere the cliff is sheer and forbidding.

Katzimo - The Enchanted Mesa. Acoma mesa to the right.

When the ancestors of the Ácomas abandoned Tapitsiama, they sought the summit of Katzimo (tradition says) through the cove in the western face, near the southern end, where the steep wall was surmounted by means of hand-and foot-holes pecked in the rock, as at Ácoma to-day. Safe from every intrusion was their new home site. With a solitary trail, so easily defended that a single man might keep an army at bay, what fear had they of enemies?

Like the other Pueblo Indians, the Ácomas have always been tillers of the soil. The fertile sands of their valley and its tributaries bore harvests of corn, beans, squashes, and cotton, the seeds of which they planted deep with a shouldered dibble, and fructified with impounded storm-water. Before the advent of the bearers of cross and sword, every man and every woman was a human beast of burden; for horsekind was unknown, and of cattle, sheep, and swine they also knew nothing. Yet, born to work, they performed the task of battling with nature for a livelihood, and performed it well; for their granaries were always full enough to enable them, if need be, to withstand a twelvemonth's siege.

Time rolled on. How long the top of Katzimo had been occupied not even the elders now know; perhaps a few generations had passed; perhaps, indeed, five hundred years had flown since the walls of Tapitsiama were left to crumble. Another springtime came, and, as of yore, the sun-priest heralded from the housetops that the time for planting was soon to come. The seeds from the last year's harvest were gathered from the bins, planting-sticks were sharpened, and the natives stood in readiness for the final announcement of the seer to repair to the fields.

Meanwhile the clans were busy in selecting representatives to participate in the great foot-races, for the Pueblos are famous runners, and, incredible as it may seem, a spirited contest over a cruel course of twenty-five miles is a feat still accomplished with comparative ease.

All was life on the mesa-top before the first eastern glow kissed with ruddy warmth the crest of Katzimo. Down the rugged trail the natives clambered—every one who was able to force a planting-stick in the compact sand, or sufficiently lithe to drive away a robber crow. Only a few of the aged and the ailing were left behind.

The sun climbed over the tinted cliff and spent its glare on the planters in the valley below. Warmer and warmer it waxed, until flecks of cloud began to appear; then new clouds formed, and they chased one another across the mesa-tops like a troop of children at play; childlike, too, their murmurings soon began, then grew louder and louder still, and the tears began to fall. The busy planters hastened in their work; but faster and faster came the rain, driving them to the shelters made of boughs and sticks from which the crops are watched. The great black dome was rent by a hundred glittering swords; the thunder crackled and roared; and the rain fell in such a torrent that Katzimo was hidden by the sky-born cataract, and the valley became a sheet of flood.

With dire forebodings the elders shook their heads. Never before had the heavens given vent to such fury. Yet as suddenly as the storm arose, so suddenly did the clouds disperse, and in all its majesty the sunlit crest of Katzimo loomed from a sea of mist.

James' party preparing for the assault on Katzimo - November, 1968.

The toilers trudged toward their mountain home. When the base of the trail was reached, huge sharp-edge blocks of stone, such as frequently fall to-day, were encountered at the talus foot, blocking the pathway of the morning, and giving mute testimony of disaster to the ladder-trail above. The Ácomas still tell us that a great rock-mass at the foot of the cove, formerly giving access to the cleft by means of the holes therein pecked, became freed from the friable wall in that memorable storm of centuries ago, and thundered downward in a thousand fragments, cutting off communication with the mesa village, and thus preventing the rescue for which the feeble voices above were calling.

Ask the Ácomas why their ancestors made no desperate effort to save from the fated town those of their flesh and blood, and they gravely shake their heads. Many a place has become enchanted to the Indian for lesser cause.

So much for the legend of la Mesa Encantada, shorn of its poetry and its pathos. When the story was first related to white people cannot be said. Perhaps it was known to the *conquistadores* who trudged the waterless sands long before Puritan feet pressed the rock of Plymouth; if so, they left no record behind. In our own time, however, the tradition was repeated to Mr. Charles F. Lummis, who resided for several years at the pueblo of Isleta, and was on intimate terms with the gray-haired priests of Ácoma.

The publication by Mr. Lummis, some twelve years ago, of the story of Katzímo aroused no little interest in the history of the giant rock among students of Southwestern ethnology—an interest which has grown apace until the very name of the Enchanted Mesa has come to be almost a household word.

Midway in the ascent through the narrow cleft where legend states the rock ladder once stood.

While conducting a reconnoissance of the pueblos of New Mexico in the summer and autumn of 1895, I visited Ácoma, where the tradition was outlined to me by Tsiki, a chief and medicine-man of renown in his tribe.

Having devoted no little time to the determination of the verity of native tradition by substantial historical and archaeological evidence, the thought of discrediting the Katzímo legend did not occur to me. During the same trip I made a visit to the great rock, three miles northeastward, and, clambering over the talus piled half-way up the cliff, entered the amphitheater through which the traditional trail had wound its way. Little difficulty was experienced in passing, unshod, over the rocky slope to within about sixty feet of the summit of the cliff; but at this point a sheer wall of thirty feet prevented further progress.

Retracing my steps, with the aid of a series of depressions that bore indication of having been artificially pecked, I rejoined my companion below, and devoted some time to an examination of the talus slope, observing that it was made up largely of earth washed from the mesa-top, scattered over which were numerous sherds of ancient pottery. The antique and the modern earthenware of the Pueblo Indians are quite distinct in texture and decoration, but the method of manufacture is identical in each case. The laborious practice of coiling, then smoothing, polishing, and painting, the clay is still in vogue; for the natives have never been initiated into the mysteries of the potter's wheel.

Not having on this occasion the facilities for climbing to the top of the mesa, I reluctantly departed from the Ácoma country, with the hope of returning and completing the examination at some future time.

Nothing more was heard of the Enchanted Mesa until last year, when it was announced in the newspapers that an expedition which had successfully reached the summit of the mesa by means of ropes shot from a life-saving mortar had, after a search of three hours, failed to find any evidence that the mesa had been inhabited in former times.

The news of the results achieved by this expedition reached me while *en route* to Arizona for the purpose of conducting some field-work in that territory. While at Moki I was directed by the Bureau of American Ethnology of the Smithsonian Institution to proceed to Ácoma and la Mesa Encantada, with a view of scaling the height, and supplementing the evidence of its former occupancy gained two years previously. The knowledge gleaned from my former trip served me well in procuring a special outfit for performing the task. I was already aware that a ladder of sufficient length to cover the thirty-foot wall, together with sufficient rope to serve as hand-lines, etc., would be all that a climb to the summit by way of the amphitheater would require. Therefore, equipped with a light extension-ladder and a sufficent quantity of half-inch rope to meet every emergency. I proceeded on the Santa Fe Pacific Railroad to the Indian village of Laguna, the most recent, yet the most rapidly decaying, of all the pueblos, where I had rare good fortune in enlisting the services of Major George H. Pradt, a civil engineer of that place; Mr. A. C. Vroman of Pasadena, California, who served as photographer; and Mr. H. C. Hayt of Chicago. To these gentlemen much of the success of the expedition is due.

Scaling the ancient rungs in the large vertical crack. Note trail of chiseled footholds on rock slope beneath climber.

The start from Laguna was not made until September 1, the day on which I had hoped to reach the mesa summit, in order that the task should be completed before the pilgrimage to Ácoma of numerous visitors from the surrounding country to witness the *Fiesta de San Estevan* on the day following; but the difficulty in obtaining a team from an Indian, who had engaged one of his brown brethren to bring in the animals from the range several days before, necessitated the postponement.

Mounted on a farm-wagon drawn by a large white horse and a mule so small that one had to look twice to be sure it was not a burro, we crept along through the suburbs of the village, where a group of Lagunas were engaged in threshing wheat by the primitive but effectual method of lashing into perpetual gallop a bunch of unshod horses set loose within a rude inclosure. The valley of the Rio San Jose, named in honor of the patron saint of Laguna, was followed for about eight miles to a point where half a dozen roads turn southward. Of these one takes his choice—they are all bad enough, and all lead to Ácoma.

It was not long before the crest of Katzímo loomed above the intervening heights; and as the valley of Ácoma was entered we looked with awe at the tremendous isolated pile, and silently wondered at the intrepidity of the Ácomas of old. After yielding to a desire to measure with our eyes the distance up the great cove near the southwestern corner, and speculating on the adequacy of our scaling equipment, we proceeded to the pueblo. A score of Navajos dashed across the sands, and made straightway, almost without slacking speed, up the horse-trail, the treacherous pitches of which have been rudely walled.

The Navajo is a veritable centaur. A tale is current in the Southwest that once an American rode a horse until apparently he could go no further; than a Mexican mounted him, and forthwith rode twenty miles more, until the poor beast fell exhausted; but a Navajo jerked him to his feet, leaped into the saddle, and won a ten-mile race!

Night came on, and belated burro-trains labored slowly in, laden with melons, peaches, and wild plums; and, between the constant proddings of their patient little beasts, the drivers bade us welcome. We made a moonlight ascent of the famous Camino del Padre, and found other preparations for the fiesta on the morrow. A flash of light across the night from a housetop-oven gave phantom outlines to the oldest dwellings in our domain, and the dying words of a herald lent a weirdness to the scene long to be remembered.

A miniature camel rock on the rugged surface of Mesa Encantada.

The start for the mesa was made early on the morning of September 3, the day after the fiesta. The sun burst through the eastern heights, and set the valley aglow with wondrous beauty. Every shrub seemed magnified, and the placid little pools, born of the storm of yesterday, glistened like diamonds in an emerald field. But the western face of Encantada looked sullen in the cool shadow of the morn, and the great cleft became a mere black gash. We pitched our camp in a clump of cedars at the base of the talus, below the amphitheater. Major Pradt immediately began the determination of the height of the cliff, which at this point proved to be 431 feet above the plain. The top of the talus was found to be 224 feet above the same point. At noon we were ready, with the aid of our two Laguna boys, to make the ascent. We shouldered the ladders, ropes, and instruments, and in a few minutes reached the top of the talus slope, very much out of breath; for the altitude of the valley is over six thousand feet, and the air is light. The real labor was yet before us; but in our anxiety to reach the top we did not tarry long before beginning to scale the steep, rocky slopes above. One of the party passed ahead, and fastened a rope to a gnarled piñon growing from the rocks through nourishment fed by the summit drainage. By this means repeated at each convenient landing-place, the other members of the party—except the two Indians, who remained below—found a safe and less arduous method of passing the treacherous pitches.

Thus was reached the narrow platform at the base of the thirty-foot wall, the highest point attained during the 1895 visit. While on this bench an interesting observation was made. In a corner of the ledge a large boulder rests, back of which a crack occurs from the top to the bottom of the thirty feet of wall. On each side of this fissure a regular series of holes had been artificially pecked for the reception of ladder-rungs; but they have been so worn away by the wash from above that they are now traceable only on close examination. Behind the boulder were found several freshly pointed oak sticks, placed there evidently by some one who had attempted to gain the summit through their agency, but had failed. Immediately afterward, almost beneath the boulder, several sherds of a modern Ácoma vessel, together with an unfeathered prayer-stick, were discovered a melancholy reminder of a votive offering made at the highest point of accessibility.

We now adjusted four of the six-foot sections of the ladder, believing that they would reach the top of the sheer wall. But the height was deceptive, and another section was added. Yet it fell short of the mark; so the last length was fitted and locked, and when the structure was raised to an almost perpendicular position the ladder reached just above the cap of the wall. To keep the ladder from slipping outward and crashing down the chasm, a hole was pecked in the soft sandstone for each leg. Again a member of the party went ahead, the remaining three holding the bottom of the ladder with all their strength. The frail structure swayed and cracked and bent like a reed, but the top of the wall was gained in safety. A rope was secured to an upper rung, and attached to a giant boulder that had found lodgment in a corner of the platform. Then the baggage, wrapped in blankets, was hauled aloft, and the remainder of the party followed, a rope being placed around the chest of each as a measure of precaution. We turned and looked out through the lofty walls of the narrow cleft across the sunny valley to the rugged *peñol* of Ácoma beyond, and the vista was one of peculiar beauty. Another perpendicular stretch of thirty feet, and the top was reached.

The passage from the deep shadow of the amphitheater, where two hours had been spent, to the sunlight of the summit, was like entering into a new world—a world like that the Ácomas entered when, as half-formed beings, they emerged from the mystic Shipápu, and began to battle anew. And what a view our eyes beheld when they had grown accustomed to the glare of this new light! A thread of blue smoke curled lazily from distant Ácoma, as if to remind us that the ancient town was weary from its yesterday's festivities. A moving speck of white across the valley green told of the departure of the last group of visitors. Away in the west, the great frowning Mesa Prieta, fringed with immense pines and skirted by the awful river of glistening black lava, overlooked the beautiful vale of Cebollita. Mount San Mateo (called Mount Taylor for the last fifty years by Americans, unaware that it had been christened a century before) loomed up in all its grandeur, the loftiest peak in New Mexico. The broken pink cliffs on every other side, at the feet of which miniature forests of piñon and cedar have served the Ácomas for fuel during generations past, walled in the beautiful grama-carpeted valley, while the whole was ceiled by a dome of turquoise festooned with clouds of burnished silver.

The rocky floor of the mesa-top had been swept and carved and swept again by the storm-demons of centuries since the "ancients" of the fleeting forms we saw on the roofs in the moonlight of the night before had descended the ladder-trail in the early morn of that fateful day.

Although the afternoon was still young, I at once saw that the remaining hours of daylight would not suffice for a thorough examination of the summit. Directing the two Lagunas below to gather together our blankets, and a sufficient supply of provisions for a couple of meals, a reconnoissance was begun, and in a few moments a fragment of greatly weather-worn ancient pottery was picked up.

The storm of the previous day, which drove the Indians from their religious ceremonies, and gave birth to the glittering little pools in the verdant valley below, afforded facilities for observation on the summit that otherwise would not have been possible. Here and there in the rocky floor "pot-holes" had been eroded by wind and rain, and were now filled with water; but nowhere else on the entire summit had the rain found resting-place. Over the brink it had poured in scores of cataracts, carrying with it stones and such earth as it managed to gather from the scanty store yet remaining. Like the mesa-dwelling Mokis of to-day, the inhabitants of Katzímo doubtless derived their water-supply from springs below—a source since hidden, either by the talus or by the Ácomas, just as springs have been covered from sight by natives at El Morro, at Tabirá, and at many other abandoned dwelling-site of old. The great cisterns of rain-water at Ácoma are unique; for nature built them in a manner far beyond native skill, and sheltered them from a thirsty sun by mighty walls of rock. Like the toiling women of Moki today, then the water-carriers of Katzímo, in all likelihood, bore their brimming *tinajas*[1] up the steep and rugged cleft, wearing deep the rocky trail of long ago.

The mesa-top was once covered with a fairly rich vegetation, piñons and cedars predominating; but most of these now stand gaunt and bare, or lie prone and decaying on the

---

1 Spanish for a large earthen jar. Anglicized in the Southwest.

bleak surface, their means of subsistence having been long washed away. A few dozen more storms, and the others must inevitably perish. But the examination of the surface of Katzímo was not essential to a determination of the fact that it was formerly mantled with a thick stratum of earth; the talus had already told the story that on the very site of their village the inhabitants of Katzímo had an abundance of material with which to make the balls of adobe mud described by one of the Spanish chroniclers of the sixteenth century. The last remnants of their houses, together with the fragments of their household utensils, save such as we found, passed over the brink generations ago; but one may still find an abundance of the latter scattered through the detritus which in places is piled half-way up the mesa sides.

From Katzímo the pine-fringed Mesa Prieta is a fitting foreground to each dying sun. Black from every point of view, it is gloomier still in the light of the ruddy mesas over which it stands guard. The sun had set, and already the moon was spreading its silvery sheen over the placid valley beneath. The smoke still curled from the drowsy village, and rose in phantom outline against the cool gray sky, the only thing of life within our range. The faint strains of a plaintive chant from the two Indians in the cedars at the foot of the great cliff increased the weirdness of our lofty camp, and almost made one wonder if it all were real. A flash of lightning made me aware of a bank of black clouds in the southwest, which sent a chilling breeze across the mesa-top. We built a huge fire around one of the gaunt specters that stood about us with outstretched arms; soon there was a mighty blaze, and a shout of approval reached us from the two Lagunas below.

The exertion of the previous afternoon, the unusual feeling that crept over us when we realized that our camp in the moonlight was pitched on the site of a honeycombed village fraught with life in the days before Columbus set sail, inspired sensations during our waking moments of the night that cannot be described. Before the red sun broke through the distant haze we were out of our blankets, and, after a hasty breakfast, each was engaged in his chosen work. While aiding Major Pradt in making a survey of the mesa-top, I was not a little surprised to find three Ácoma Indians among us. They were by no means friendly at first; for, having seen our fire the night before, they had come to the top by means of our ladders to learn the cause of this unusual burst of flame from their ancestral home site, and to oust the intruders from the height. The leader, who was the war chief of the tribe, and a medicine-man, asked us our business. We told him. The natives became interested, and said that their people had feared we were after their land. Being assured we had no desire to make our future home on their dry sand-dunes or drier mesas, but that we were merely looking for pottery fragments, the chief expressed serious doubt that any relics could be found, inasmuch as many ages had passed since his people lived on the great table, and he believed all evidences of former occupancy had been swept or washed away. The interest of the three Indians were quite apparent when I showed them the fragment of pottery picked up by Major Pradt the evening before, and they manifested no unwillingness to search for other potsherds when I made the suggestion. They were engaged in this quest only a short while when they returned with several fragments of extremely ancient, greatly worn earthenware, a large projectile-point, a portion of a shell bracelet, and parts of two grooved stone axes, all lichen-flecked with age, and still moist from contact with the ground. Thoroughly satisfied with the outcome, I decided to bring the work to a close as soon as the survey, the photographic work, and the examination of the general features of the mesa's summit were concluded.

When I considered that the summit of Katzímo is, and long has been, absolutely inaccessible to the Indians; that it has been washed by rains and swept by winds for centuries, until scarcely any soil is left on its crest, as the bare trees plainly attest; that numberless blocks of soft sandstone, weighing hundreds of tons, have so recently fallen from the cliff that their edges have not had time to become rounded by erosion; that the topography of the summit is such that not a cupful of water now remains on the surface, save in a few eroded pot-holes in the sandstone, but that it rushes over the precipice on every side in a hundred cataracts; that well-defined traces of an ancient ladder-trail may still be seen, pecked in the rocky wall of the very cleft through which the traditional pathway wound its course; and, above all, the large numbers of very ancient potsherds in the earthy talus about the base of the mesa, which must have been washed from above—the conclusion was inevitable that the summit of la Mesa Encantada was inhabited prior to 1540, when the present Ácoma was discovered by Coronado, and that the last vestige of the village itself has long been washed or blown over the cliff.

As we wended our way across the arroyo-scarred plain, I still looked in awe at the royal height, and wondered again at the Ácomas of old.

View from the top. Looking west over the great Acoma valley.

And so, at every turn, there are hints and flashes of the unknown and the unknowable, the pettiest of which you shall try in vain to fathom. Their marvelous mythology, their infinitely complicated social, religious and political economies, their exhaustless and beautiful folklore—of all, you shall everywhere find clues, but nowhere knowledge. And as the rumbling farm wagon jolts you back from your enchanted dream to the prosy wide-awake of civilization, you shall go to be forever haunted by that unearthly cliff, that weird city, and their unguessed dwellers.

Lummis
Land of Poco Tiempo
P. 76